IMAGES
My first picture book

Pictures:
Yvette Barbetti, Christian Galinet, Héliadore,
Bruno Le Sourd, Michel Loppé,
Frankie Merlier, Geneviève Monjaret,
Aline Riquier, Catherine Siegel,

Double-page illustrations:
Philip Horton and Tricia Lengyel

FLEURUS

What do we put on bread at breakfast? What do we make with fruit and sugar?

butter

sugar

jam

chocolate

coffee beans

What is bad for our teeth if we eat too much of it?

What do we eat with a spoon?

yogurt

cereal

lollipops

candies

hamburger

What do we find at the delicatessen?

What do we find at the bakery?

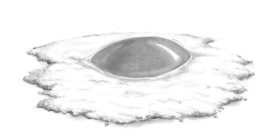

fried egg

bread

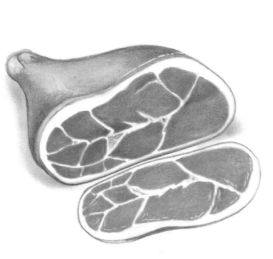

ham

pasta

What can we make with potatoes? Point to the shellfish.

mashed potatoes

fish

French fries

oyster

mussel

What do we find at the supermarket?

What do we eat with maple syrup?

meat

cheese

chicken

pancakes

waffles

What is cold and delicious? What do we bake with fruit?

an ice-cream

doughnuts

a cookie

a tart

What do we pick from a vine? Which fruit can we squeeze for juice?

a cake

a lemon

a bunch of grapes

an orange

Which fruit grows on a pear tree, a peach tree, an apple tree and a plum tree?

Which fruit's juice do we use to make cider?

a pear

a peach

an apple

plums

Which fruit grows on an orange tree?

Which fruit does not grow on trees?

an apricot

a melon

a mandarin orange

a grapefruit

Which fruits grow in hot countries?

What wild fruit can we find growing in the country?

a pineapple

blackberries

a banana

raspberries

In which fruit do we find pits?

What is a squirrel's favorite food?

cherries

blueberries

strawberry

hazelnuts

What has a very hard shell? Which vegetable can we eat with our fingers?

a walnut

asparagus

olives

celery

Which garden vegetable is purple?

Which vegetables do we cut into round slices to eat?

a zucchini

a red pepper

an eggplant

a cucumber

Which vegetable do we use to make fries?

Which vegetable's leaves do we eat?

a potato

a tomato

a carrot

an artichoke

Which vegetable has yellow seeds?

Which vegetable do we preserve in a jar with vinegar?

a corn cob

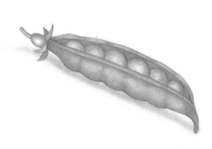

peas

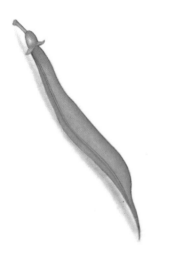

a green bean

a gherkin

Which vegetables have large green leaves? Which vegetable is small, pink and white?

a cauliflower

a lettuce

a cabbage

a radish

In the garden

Let's see how many things
we can find

What makes us cry when we peel it?

What can grow either in a mushroom bed or in the woods?

an onion

a pumpkin

garlic

a mushroom

What do we slide on?

Where do we find a trapeze, a swing and some rings?

smoke

chimney

roof

window

door

shutter

a house

a swing set

a slide

a bench

What do we need when we have to reach things which are too high?

Where do we put the dishes in the kitchen?

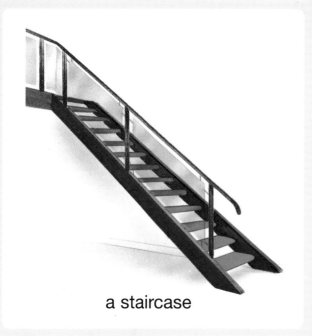

a staircase

a cupboard

a ladder

a step-ladder

Where should we put food to keep it cool?

In what would we wash the family's clothes?

a vacuum cleaner

a washing machine

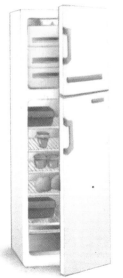

a refrigerator

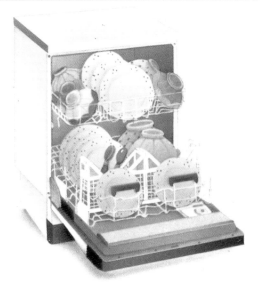

a dishwasher

In what do we bake delicious cakes?

Where do we make coffee for breakfast?

an oven

a stove

a food processor

a sink

an electric coffee maker

What do we use to weigh the flour to make a big cake?

Where do we fry eggs?

a toaster

saucepans

scales

a frying pan

What do we use to bake little cakes?

Where do we warm up frozen foods?

a casserole dish

a pressure-cooker

cake pans

a microwave oven

What do we put on the table when we set it?

Where do we put the gravy to bring it to the table?

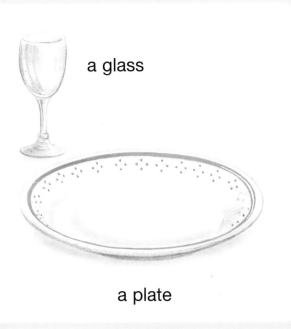

a glass

a plate

a small spoon

a big spoon

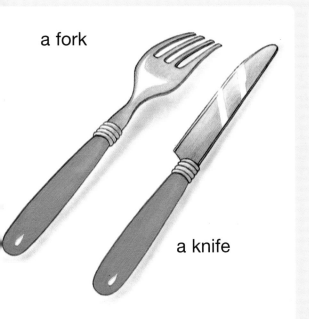

a fork

a knife

a gravy boat

a dish

In what do we serve the soup, and what do we use to pour it into soup bowls? What do we use at breakfast time?

a salad bowl

a bowl

a cup

a ladle

a soup tureen

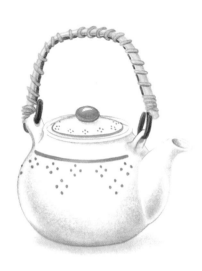

a teapot

What does Mom use to carry her shopping? Where do we put salt and pepper?

a shopping cart

a bottle

a colander

a pepper mill   a salt-shaker

In the kitchen

Let's find as many things
as possible

What do we use to open bottles? What do we use to light the gas?

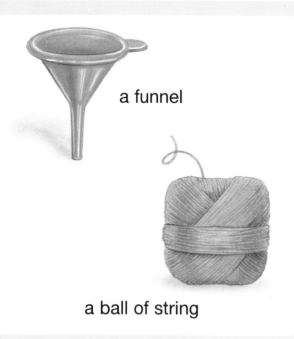

a funnel

a ball of string

a cork

a corkscrew

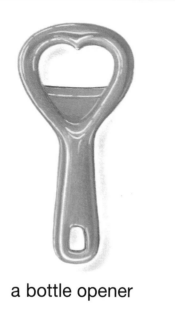

a bottle opener

a gas-lighter

a match

What do we need to do
the ironing?

Where do we throw away
the rubbish?

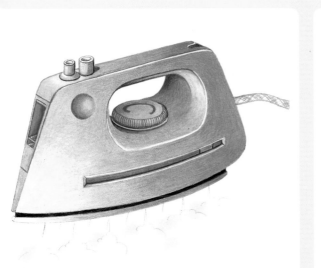

an iron

a dustpan

a broom

an ironing board

a waste basket

What do we put on the table to make it look pretty?

What do we use to hang out the washing?

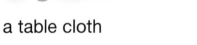
table napkins

a table cloth

a bowl

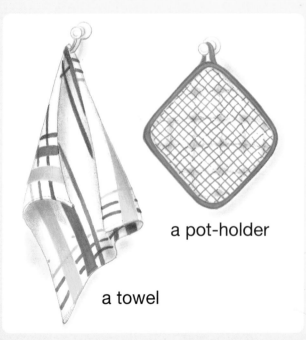

a pot-holder

a towel

a clothes pin

What tells us the time?

What can we sit on?

a clock

a chair

a light-bulb

a lamp

a stool

Where do we put away books? Where do we sit down to relax?

a table

an armchair

a bookcase

a sofa

What warms up the house? Where do we put away our toys?

a radiator

a chest of drawers

a carpet

a toy chest

What do we need on our beds to make us comfortable?

Where do we put away our clothes?

a pillow

a quilt

a bed

a wardrobe

a bedside table

a desk

On what do we put a baby to go to the bathroom?

What do we use to brush our hair?

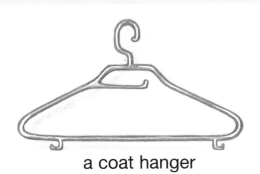

a coat hanger

a clothes brush

a face cloth

a towel

a potty

a hairbrush

a comb

What do we use to brush our teeth every morning?

What do we use to wash?

a nail brush

a bar of soap

toothpaste

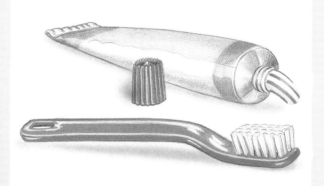

a toothbrush

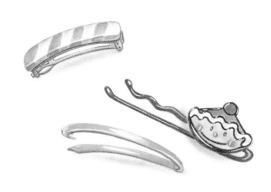

barrettes

What makes lots of bubbles when we wash our hair? What do we use to take our temperature when we are sick?

shampoo

a thermometer

an electric razor

a hair dryer

Where do we put away our toothbrush, hairbrush and other things?

Where do we take a bath?

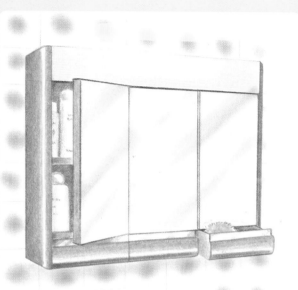

a bathroom cabinet

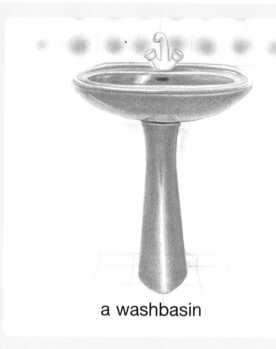

a washbasin

a clothes rack

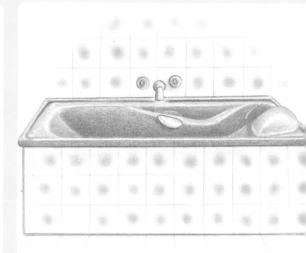

a bath tub

What do we find in a bathroom? What do we wear if we can't see very well?

a toilet

a pair of glasses

a shower

an umbrella

In the bedroom

Let's find as many things
as possible

What do we do with these? What do we wear on our wrist that tells us the time?

a mirror

a clock

a lighter

a wristwatch

Where can we read some interesting stories?

Where do we put a letter before mailing it?

a newspaper

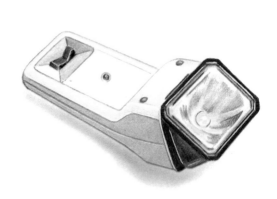

a flashlight

a book

an envelope

What do we use to lock and unlock doors?

What do we use to speak to someone far away?

a key

a picture

a vase

a telephone

What rings in the morning to wake us up at the right time? Where do we put our clothes before we go on a vacation?

an alarm clock

an aquarium

a birdcage

a suitcase

What can we use to carry water when we go for a walk?

What looks like a little girl?

a plastic bottle

a doll

building blocks

a teddy bear

What can we use to play cowboys?

Which toy helps us to learn how to pedal?

a horse on wheels

a tricycle

a scooter

hand-puppets

What do we use to knock over bowling pins

What do we put on our feet to go fast?

bowling pins

a bowling ball

roller-skates

marbles

a game of darts

What do we need to feed a doll?

What do we call a picture cut up into pieces?

a ball

a jigsaw puzzle

a tea-set

a picture book

Where would we find a diamond, a club, a heart and a spade?

What do we fly in the sky when it's windy?

playing cards

a bucket

a spade

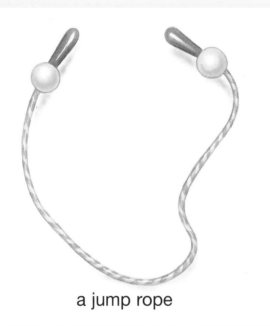

a jump rope

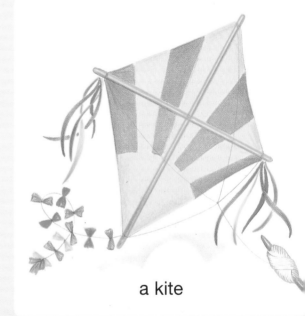

a kite

Where do we put our things to go to school?

What do we use to draw colorful pictures?

a book bag

a pencil

a pencil case

colored pencils

What do we use to measure and to draw straight lines?

What do we use to erase drawings on paper?

a felt-tip pen

an eraser

a ruler

a pencil sharpener

With what do we write on a blackboard?

What do we need to paint beautiful colored pictures?

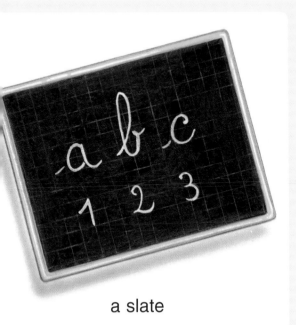

a slate

a notebook

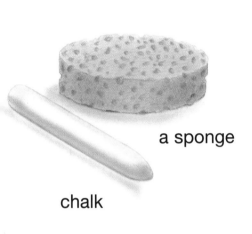

a sponge

chalk

a paint box

a paintbrush

What makes things bigger so we can see them better? What do we use to take small children for a walk?

a magnifying glass

a playpen

a pen

a stroller

What do we use to take very small babies for a walk?

Where do we sit a baby to feed him?

a baby carriage

a crib

a bassinet

a baby chair

Where do we put the milk to feed a baby?

What do babies wear to keep them dry?

a mobile

a diaper

a bottle

a vest

What do we put on a baby to keep his clothes clean when he eats?

What do girls sometimes wear at night to sleep in?

a bib

bootees

baby pajamas

a nightdress

What do boys wear to sleep in?

What color is the dress?

a robe

a dress

pajamas

pants

What do we wear to play sports?

What do we wear to go out when it's cold in winter?

a skirt

an overcoat

overalls

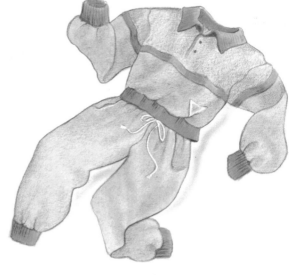

a tracksuit

What do we wear indoors to keep us warm?

If we play winter sports, what do we wear to keep us warm in the snow?

a sweater

a jacket

an undershirt

an anorak

What do boys wear?
What do girls wear?

What do boys and girls wear to go swimming?

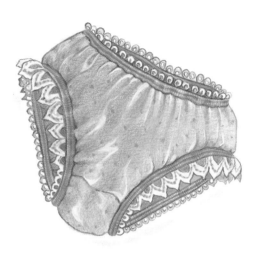

panties

shorts

underwear

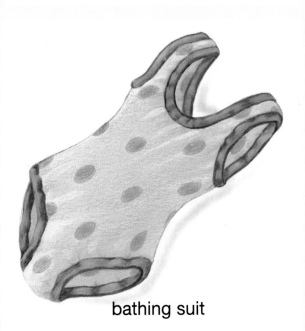

bathing suit

When it rains, what should we wear to stay dry?

What do we slip onto our feet before we put on our shoes?

a t-shirt

a raincoat

a shirt

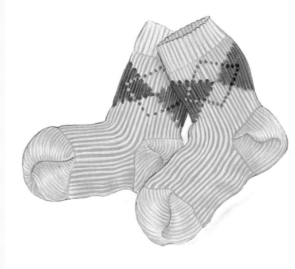

socks

When it's cold, what do we put on to keep our heads and necks warm?

What do we put on our hands to keep the cold out?

hat

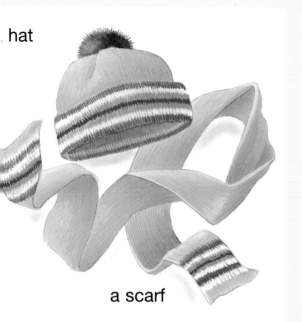

a scarf

mittens

gloves

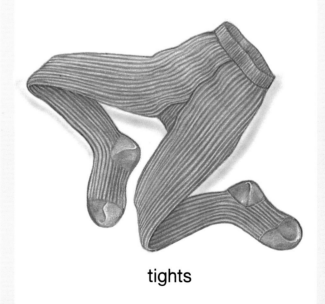

tights

What do we wear on our feet inside the house?

What do we wear on our feet when it rains so that we can splash in the puddles?

sneakers

boots

slippers

shoes

What do we wear to hold up our pants?

What do we carry in our pockets when we have a cold?

a baseball cap

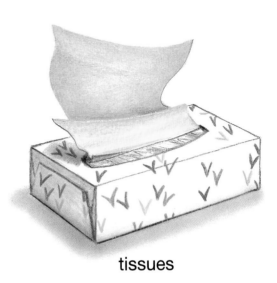

tissues

suspenders

a belt

In the park

Let's find as many things as possible

What piece of jewelry do we wear around our neck?

What do we put in the tape player so that we can listen to music?

a necklace

earrings

a ring

a wedding ring

bracelets

a cassette

What can we take with us to listen to music while we're out for a walk?

In which machine do we put cassettes to listen to music?

a compact disc

a stereo system

a portable CD player

a radio-cassette player

Which machine do we use to make videos? What do we use to take photos?

a camcorder

a camera

a VCR

a computer

Which machine allows us to watch cartoons?

If we don't know how to swim, what do we need in the water?

a typewriter

a beach umbrella

a television

a rubber ring

What do we put on our feet to be able to slide along the snow? And on the ice?

What would we use to get high up in the mountains without having to walk?

ski poles

skis

a toboggan

a cable-car

ice skates

What do we use when we play tennis?

What do we use to fish in the river?

a ping-pong ball

table tennis paddles

a tent

a tennis ball

a tennis racket

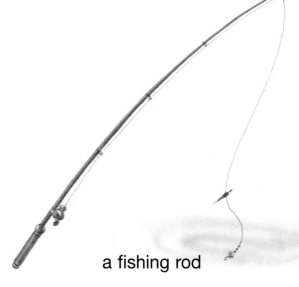

a fishing rod

What speeds along the water using the power of the wind?

Which boats need oars to move?

a windsurfer

a rubber boat

a sailboat

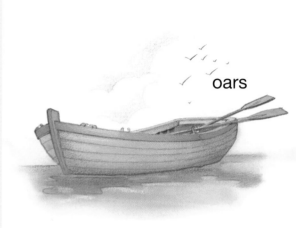

oars

a row boat

What allows us to fly in the sky like a bird? What do we use when we want to see something which is far away?

a parachute

a knapsack

a hang-glider

a pair of binoculars

Which instruments have strings to make music?

Which instrument has a keyboard with black and white notes?

a bow   a violin

an electronic keyboard

a guitar

a xylophone

Which instruments do we blow in to make music? What do we use to dig the garden?

a tambourine

a trumpet

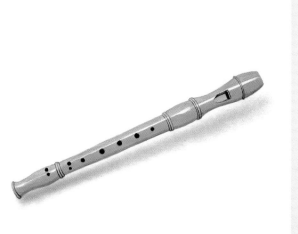

a recorder

a garden fork

What do we use to carry earth? What do we use to cut long grass?

a rake

a lawn mower

a wheelbarrow

clippers

What do we carry water for the plants in?

What tool do we use to pull out nails?

a watering can

a shovel

a hammer

pliers

What do we use to put in screws?

Which machine makes holes in the wall?

a screwdriver

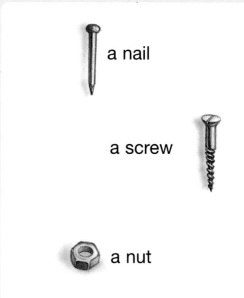

a nail

a screw

a nut

a wrench

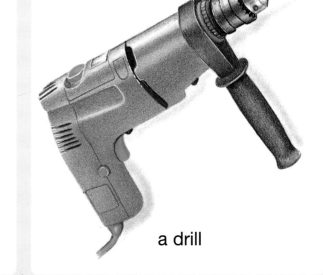

a drill

What tools do we use to cut wood?

What tool do we need to measure an object?

a saw

a tape measure

an axe

a level

What do we need to sew on a button?

What do we use to cut paper or cloth?

a spool of thread

a needle

a safety pin

a button

a pair of scissors

a thimble

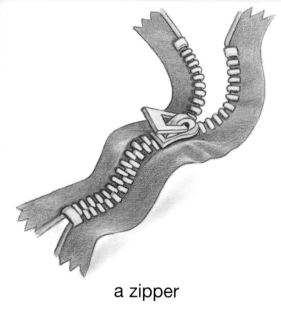

a zipper

What do we need to make a sweater?

What color is the traffic light that makes the cars stop?

a ball of wool

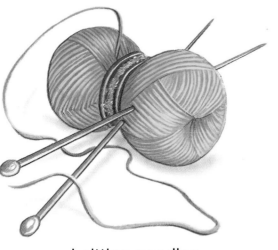

knitting needles

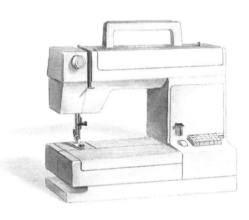

a sewing machine

a sampler

a traffic-light

Which vehicle can carry lots of people at the same time?

What sort of truck can transport gas?

a car

a truck

a bus

a tanker

When we are big, what do we ride on after we've learned to ride a tricycle?

What should we wear on our head when we ride a motor-cycle?

a bicycle

a helmet

a motorcycle

a moped

What do we use to pump up bicycle tires?

What can lift very heavy objects at a building site?

a cycle pump

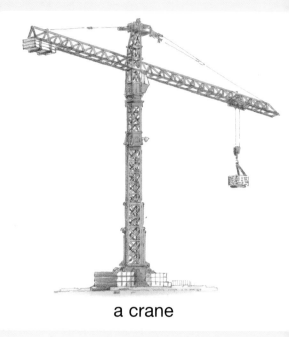

a crane

a tire

a digger

What does the farmer use to harvest the wheat?

What can we tow behind a car to go on vacation?

a bulldozer

a trailer

a combine-harvester

a tractor

What travels on rails and goes very fast?

What flies high in the sky and carries lots of passengers?

a train

a helicopter

a boat

an airplane

What do astronauts use to travel in space?

What shines in the sky at night?

a rocket

the sun

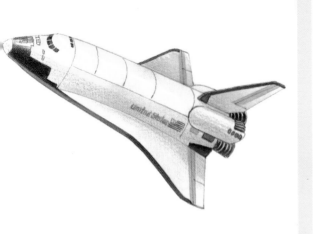

a space-shuttle

the stars

the moon

Transportation

Let's find as many things
as possible

When it has stopped raining and the sun comes out, what can we see in the sky?

What appears on the branches of a tree in spring?

clouds

a rainbow

a tree

a fire

leaves

a branch

What hides away inside a prickly shell during the autumn?

Which nut can you eat?

a coconut

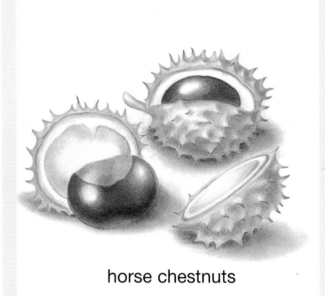

horse chestnuts

a pine cone

acorns

What prickly plant do we use to decorate the house at Christmas?

What color is the daffodil?

a rose

a cornflower

holly

a daffodil

What is the name of the red flower often found in gardens in spring?

Which flower has the name of a food in it?

a poppy

a daisy

a buttercup

a tulip

Which flowers do we buy when we want to make a lovely display? Which is the first flower to appear in the spring?

a petunia

a geranium

a primrose

a carnation

What color is the pansy?

Which flowers do we often find in the middle of the lawn?

an anemone

a nasturtium

a pansy

dandelions

Which flowers are purple? Which flowers are white?

violets

a crocus

lily of the valley

a hyacinth

Which plant is covered in prickles and doesn't need water?

Which bird sits on a perch and sometimes talks a lot?

an iris

a thistle

a cactus

a parrot

Which bird sings at dawn? Which bird often builds its nest under the eaves of a house?

a crow

a sparrow

a blackbird

a swallow

Which bird lives near the sea? Which bird has a pretty red breast?

a magpie

a robin

a seagull

a pigeon

109

Which bird sleeps during the day and wakes up at night? Which animal has no feet?

an eagle

a crocodile

an owl

a snake

What is the difference between a bactrian camel and a dromedary?

Which animal loves to eat honey and fish?

a bactrian camel

a bear

a panda

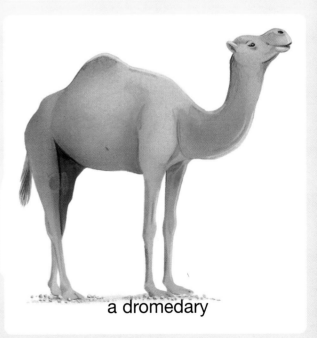

a dromedary

Which animal loves making faces?

Which animal is called the king of the jungle?

a leopard

a lion

a tiger

a monkey

Which animal has four legs and a very long neck?

Which is the heaviest of all the animals? It has four legs and huge white tusks.

a giraffe

an elephant

a hippopotamus

a rhinoceros

Which animal has a pouch in its stomach to carry its baby? Which animal looks like a horse in striped pajamas?

a kangaroo

a gazelle

a zebra

an ostrich

Which sea animal is sometimes trained to play with balls? Which animal lives in the sea and is bigger and heavier than a truck?

a penguin

a whale

a dolphin

a seal

Which animals have large claws at the end of their legs and live on the sea-floor?

What small sea creature do we eat?

a lobster

a shrimp

a crab

a swan

Which bird sometimes makes its nest on top of chimneys? Which animal builds dams in the river?

a stork

a beaver

a frog

a guinea pig

Which animal loves nibbling cheese and bread? Which animal likes to go out in the rain and carries a shell on its back?

a mouse

a snail

a slug

a turtle

Which animal lies on stones and basks in the sun?

Which animal is told to 'fly away home' and is usually seen in the summer?

a worm

a grasshopper

a lizard

a ladybug

Which animal is a caterpillar before it grows up?

Which insect buzzes as it flies, and gives a nasty bite?

an ant

a fly

a butterfly

a mosquito

Which insect lives in a hive and makes honey?

Which insect spins a web to catch other insects and then eats them?

a wasp

a spider

a hive

a bee

a dragonfly

Which animal turns into a beautiful butterfly?

Which animal loves eating nuts?

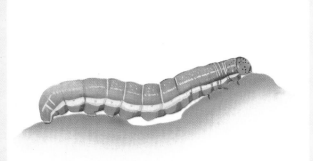

a caterpillar

a squirrel

a hare

a porcupine

What are the fawn's parents called?

Which animal is said to be very sly?

a fawn

a doe

a stag

a fox

Which animal looks like a dog but lives in the forest and howls?

Which animal sleeps in a small house and loves eating bones?

a wolf

a cat

a wild boar

a bone   a dog

Which stubborn animal can we ride on?

Which birds like to splash in the pond?

a donkey

a duck

a duckling

a rabbit

a drake

What is the baby hen or rooster called?

Which animal crows first thing in the morning and wakes up the farm?

a goose

a hen   a chick

a turkey

a rooster

Which animals give us milk?

Which animal has a pink skin, often covered in mud?

a goat

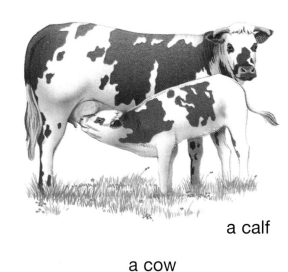

a calf

a cow

a pig

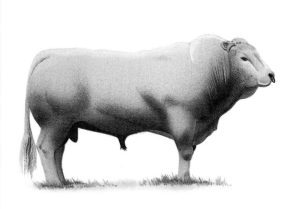

a bull

Which animal provides the wool to make warm sweaters?

a sheep

a lamb

a horse

a foal

THEMATIC CONTENTS

PICTURE SCENES

INDEX

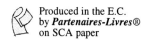
Produced in the E.C.
by *Partenaires-Livres*®
on SCA paper

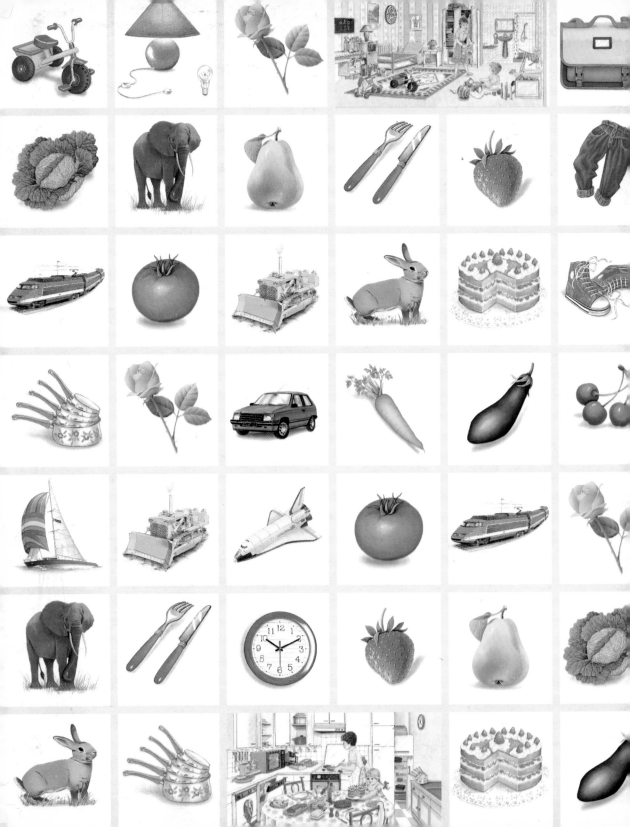